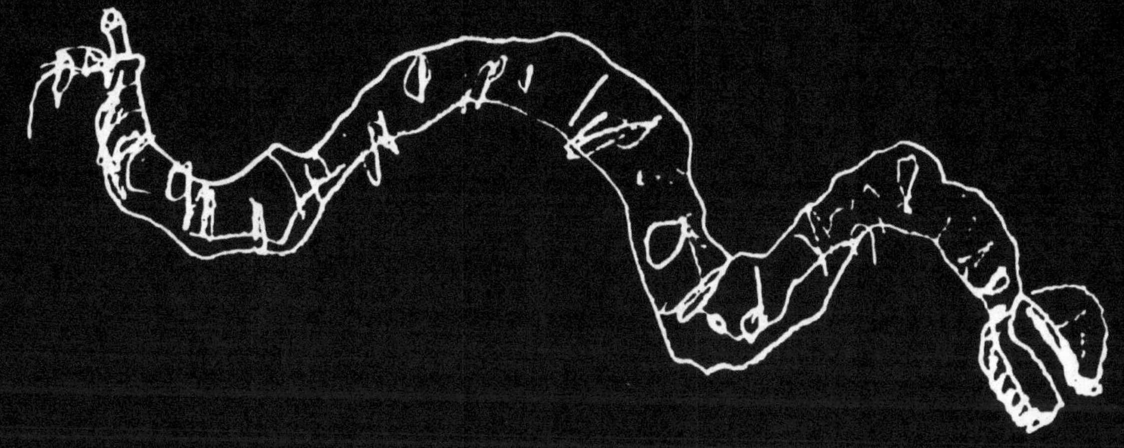

# HAUNTED ROBOT FACTORY

By

justin AERNI

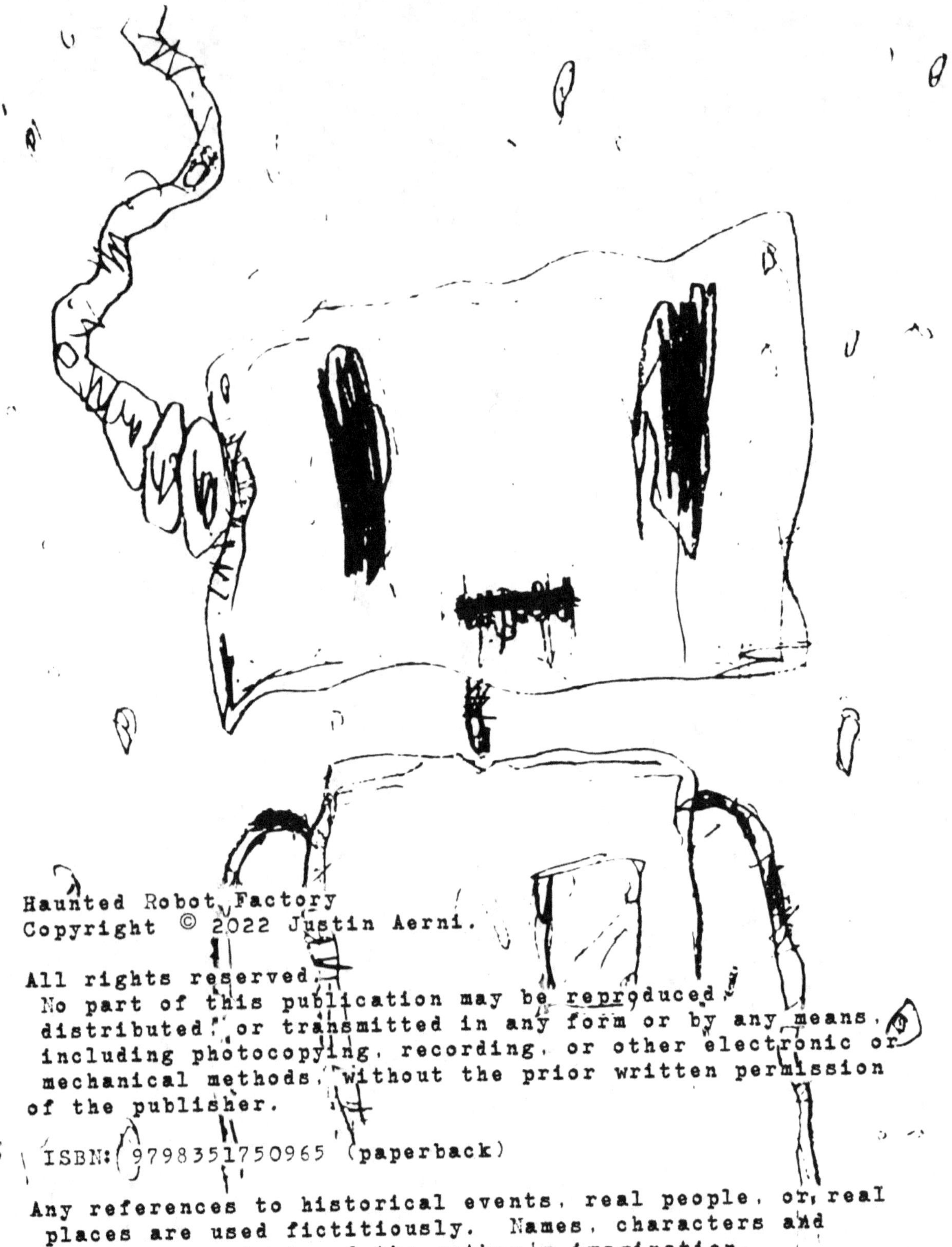

Haunted Robot Factory


ISBN: 9798351750965 (paperback)

Any references to historical events, real people, or real places are used fictitiously. Names, characters and places are products of the author's imagination.

Front cover, book design & interior art all by Justin Aerni.
First printing edition 2022.
www.aerniart.com

# HAUNTED ROBOT FACTORY

ADULT COLORING BOOK

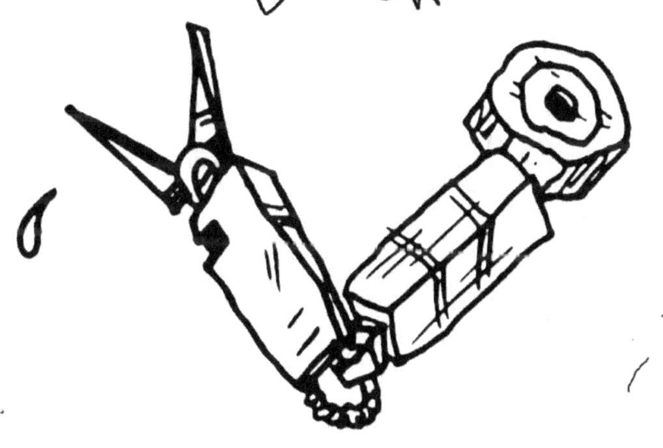

BY JUSTIN AERNI

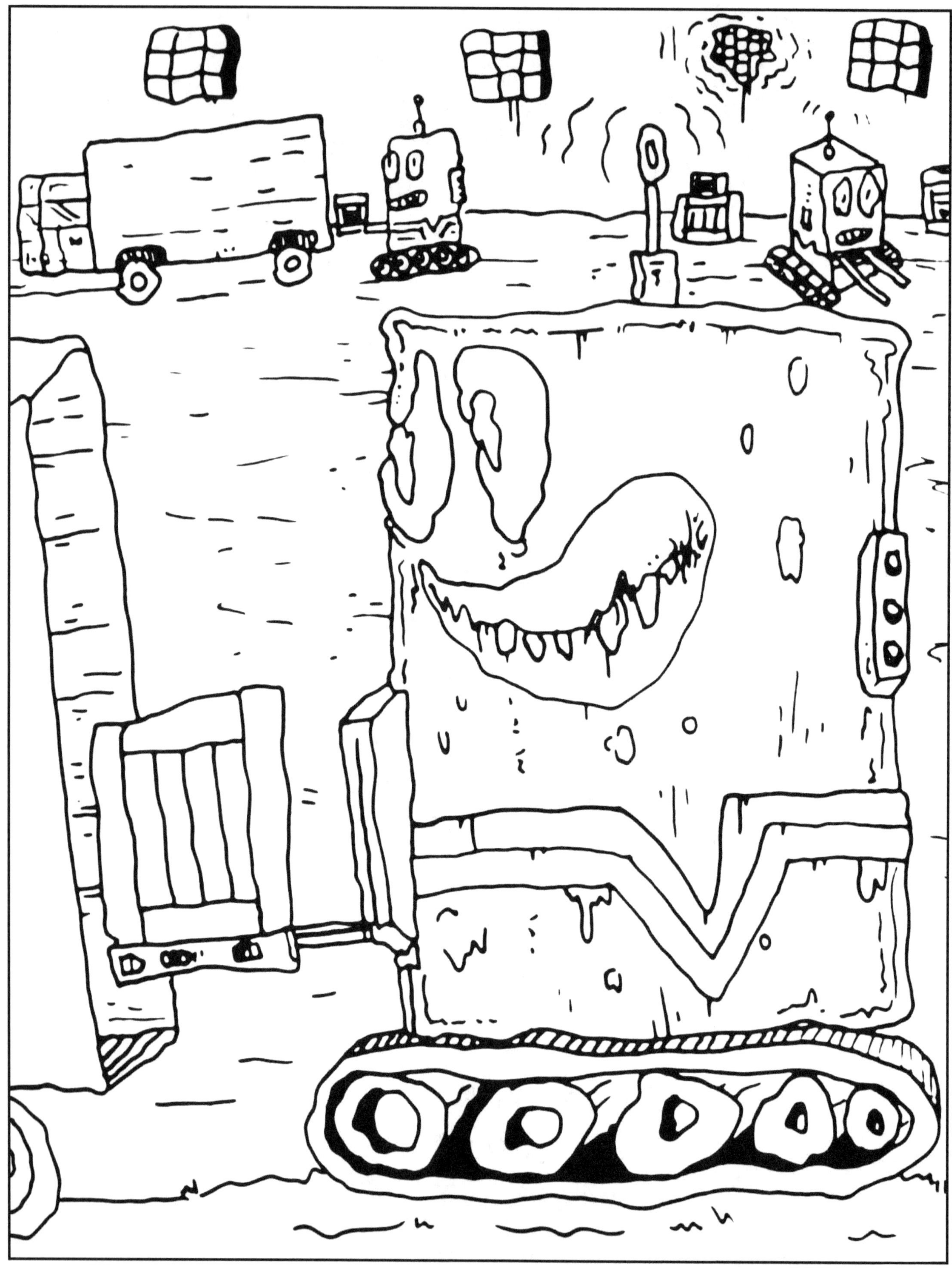

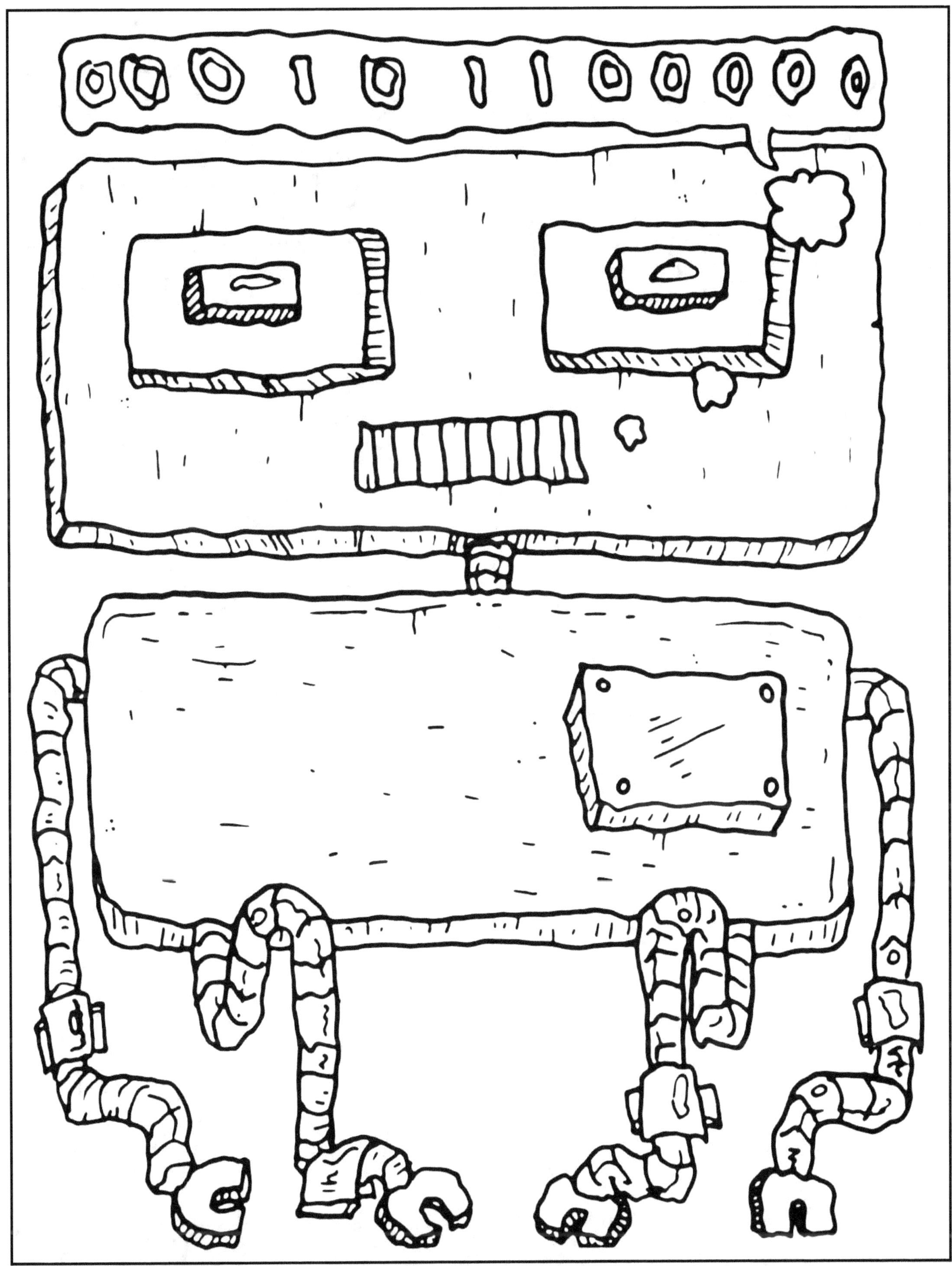
000101100000

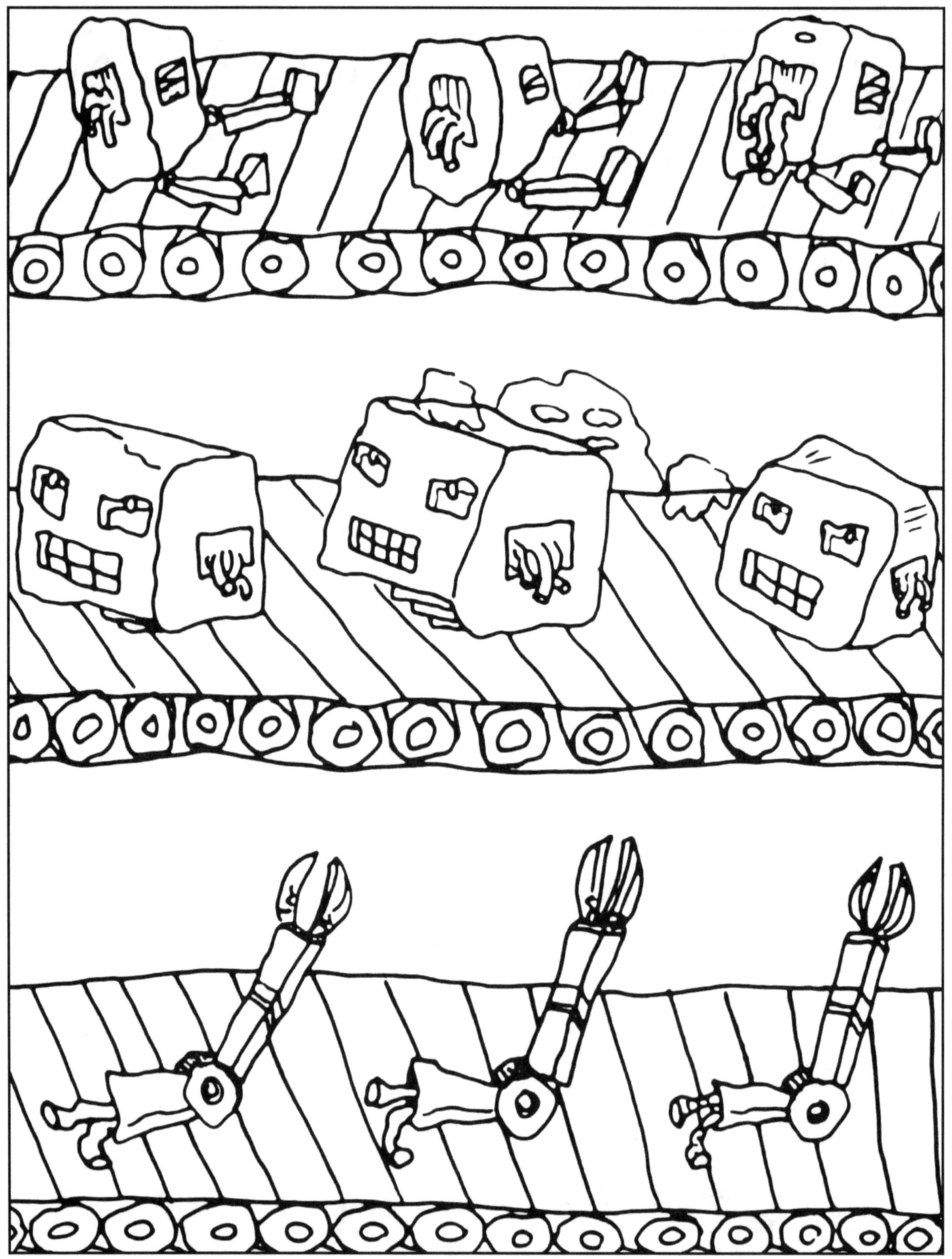

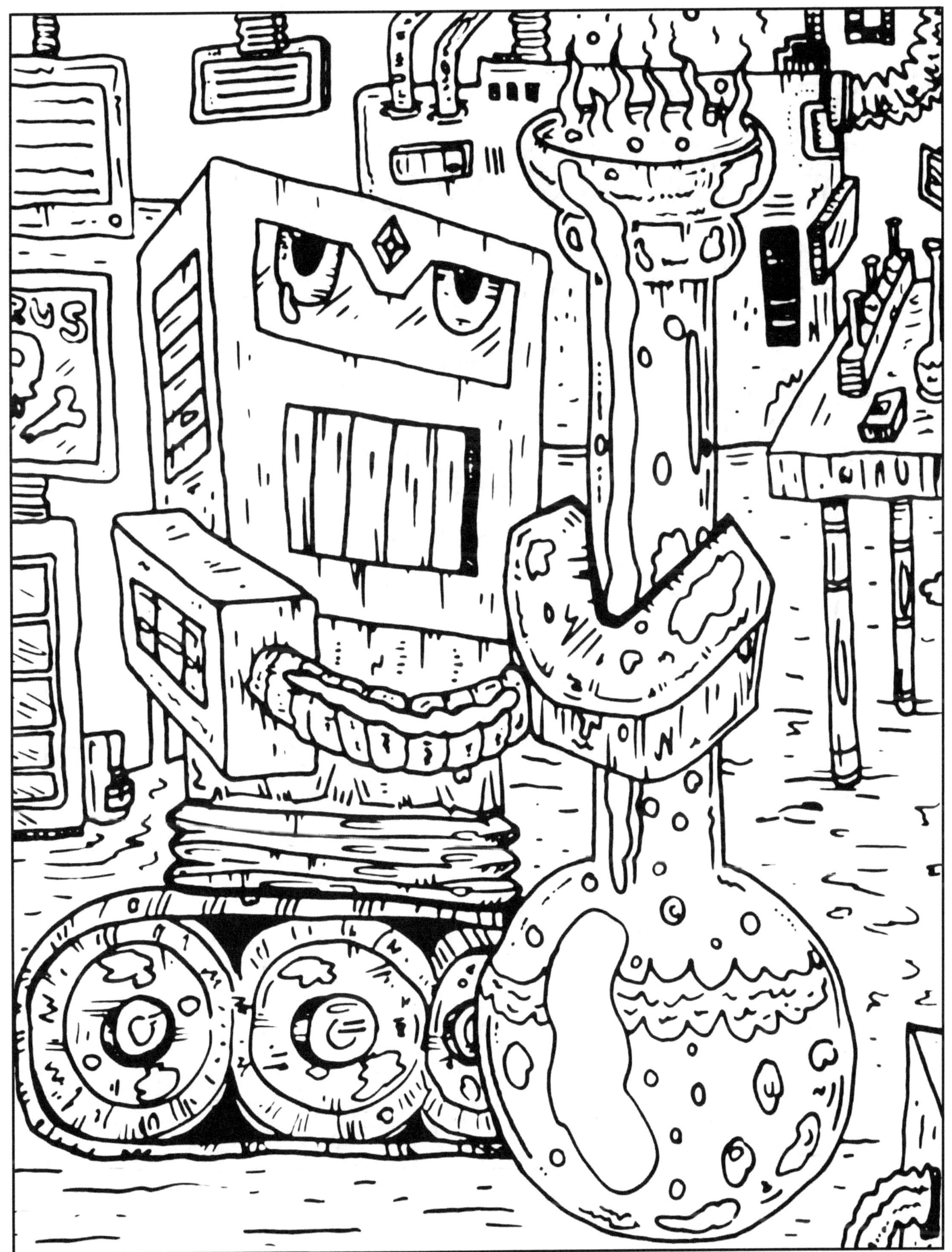

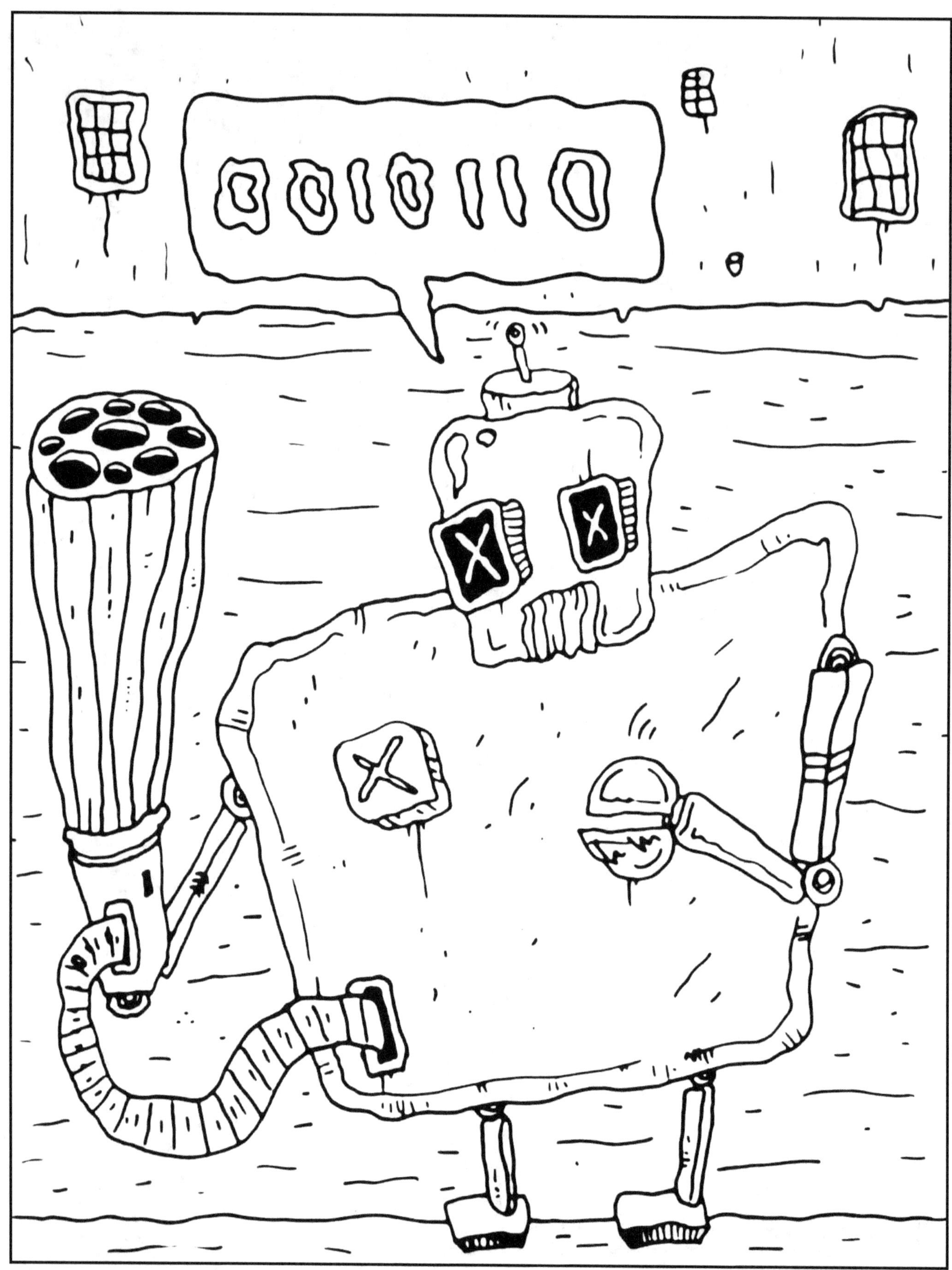
0010110

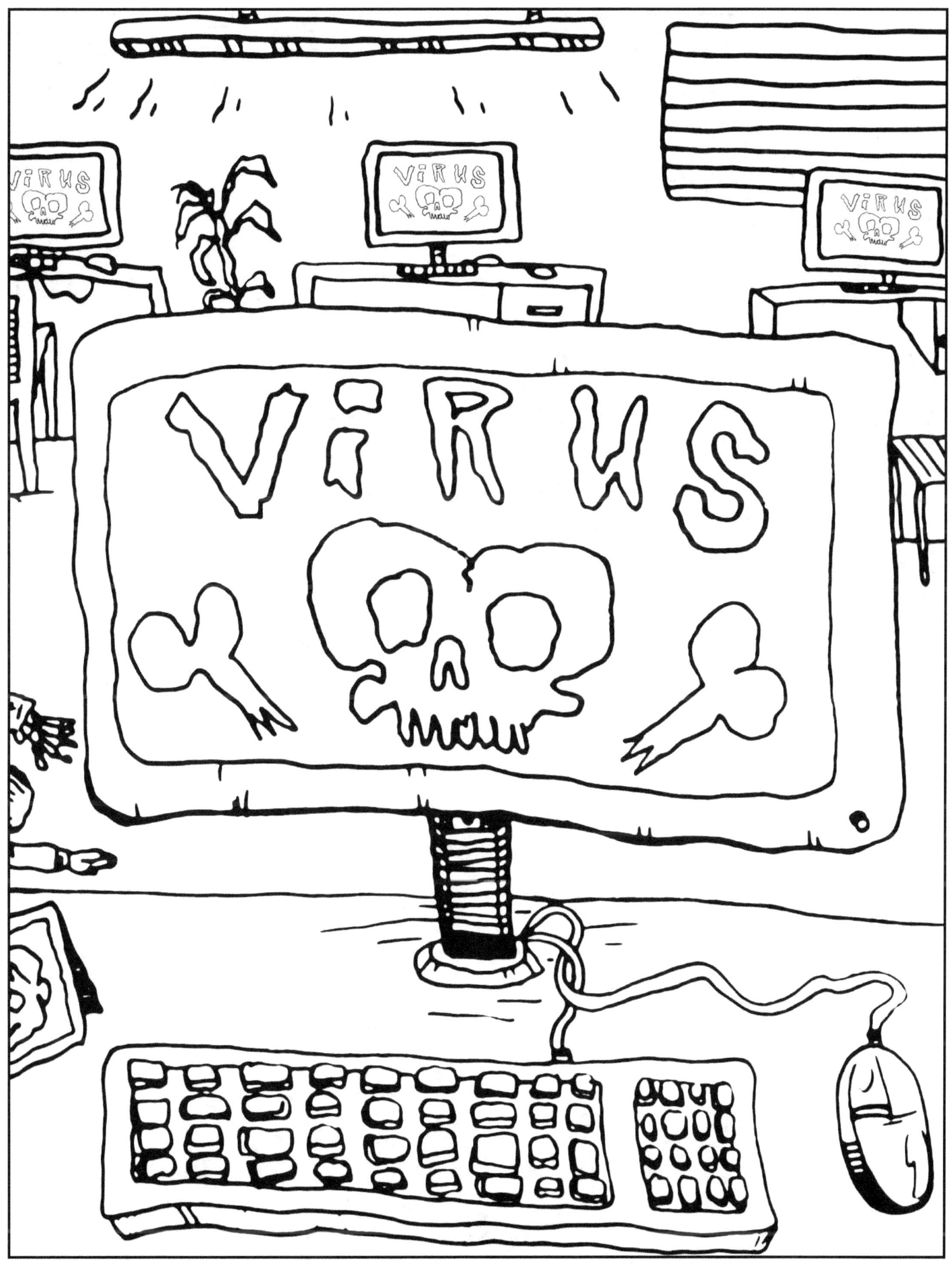
ViRUS
ViRUS
ViRUS
ViRUS

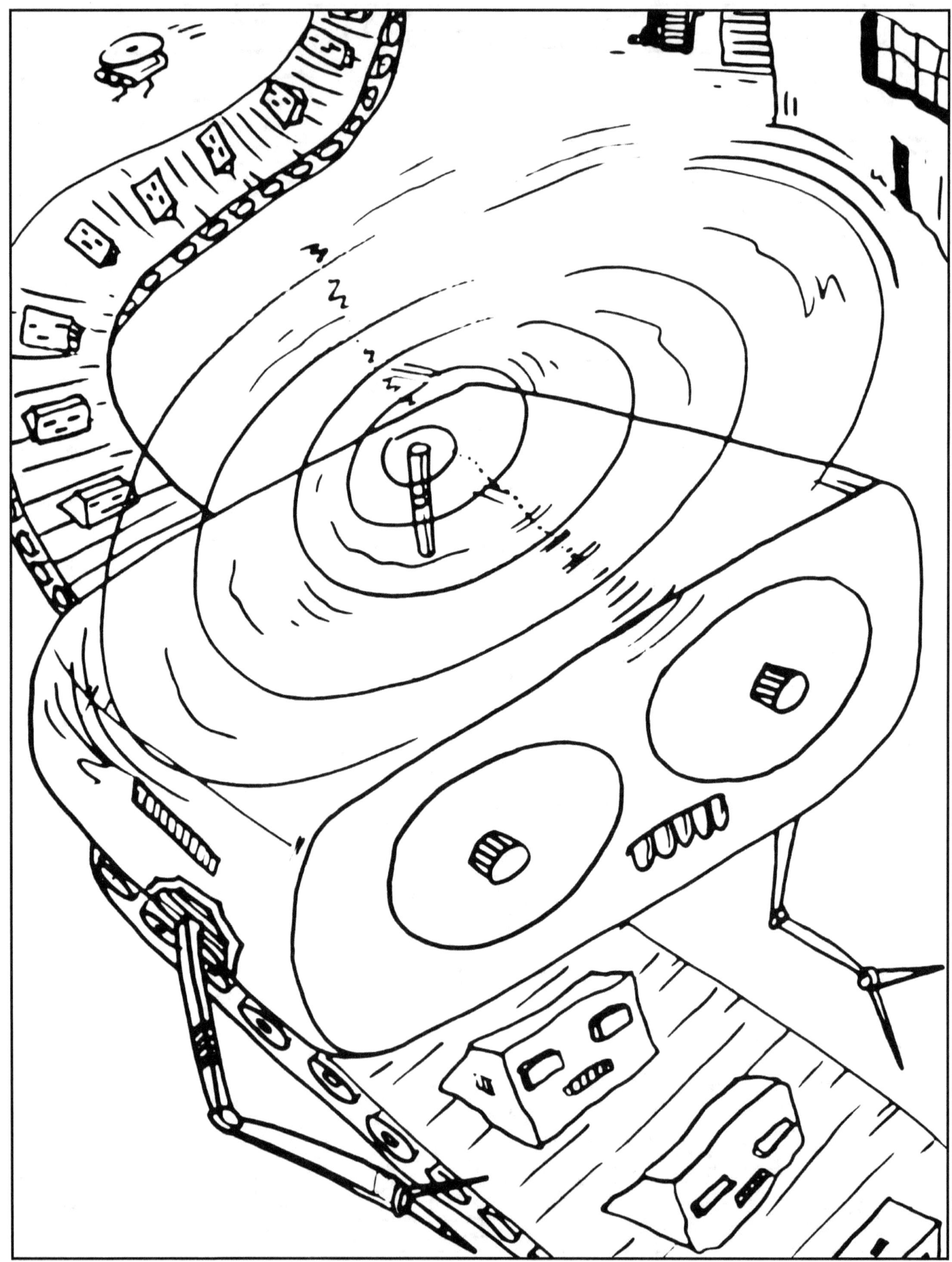

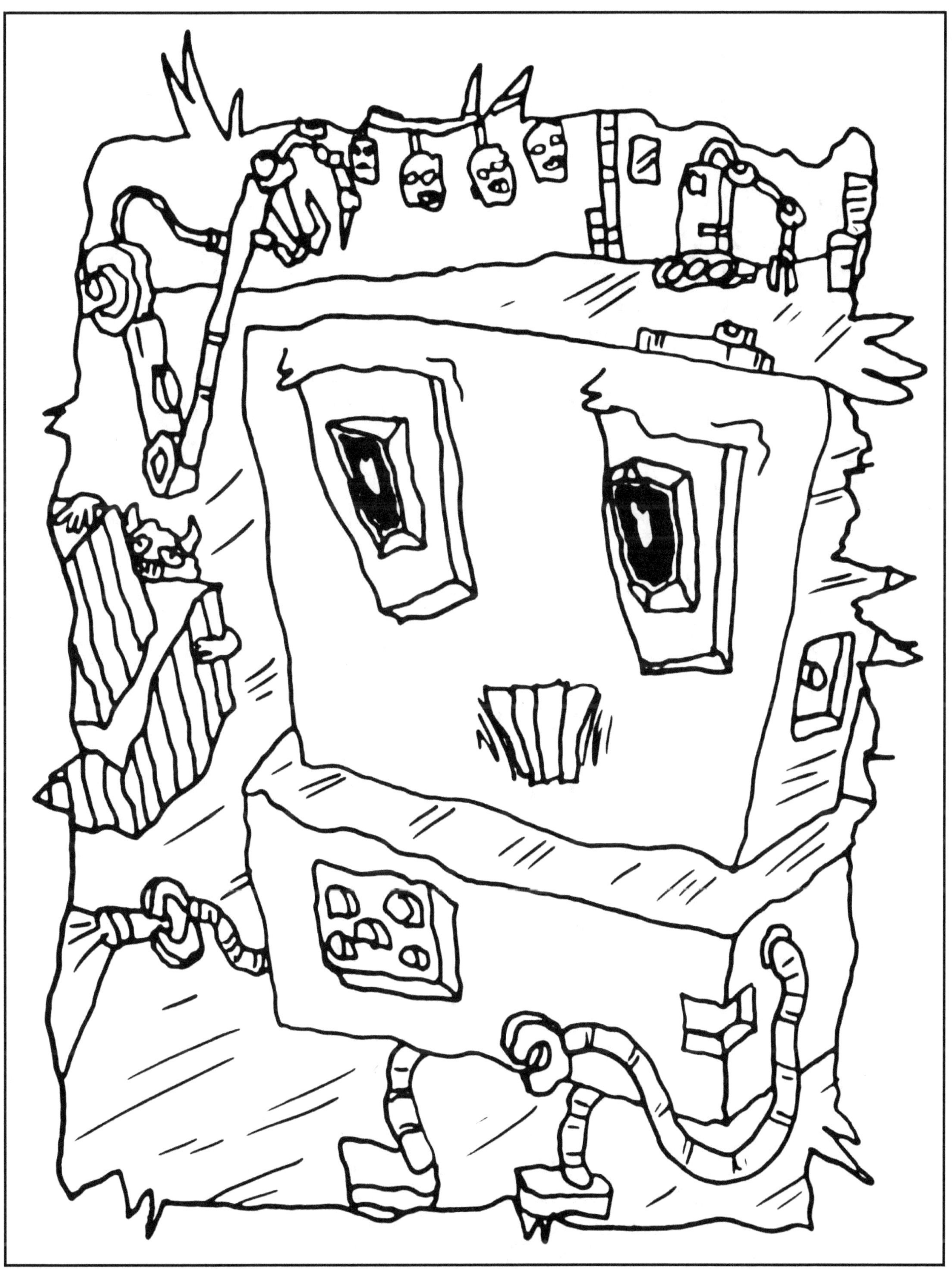

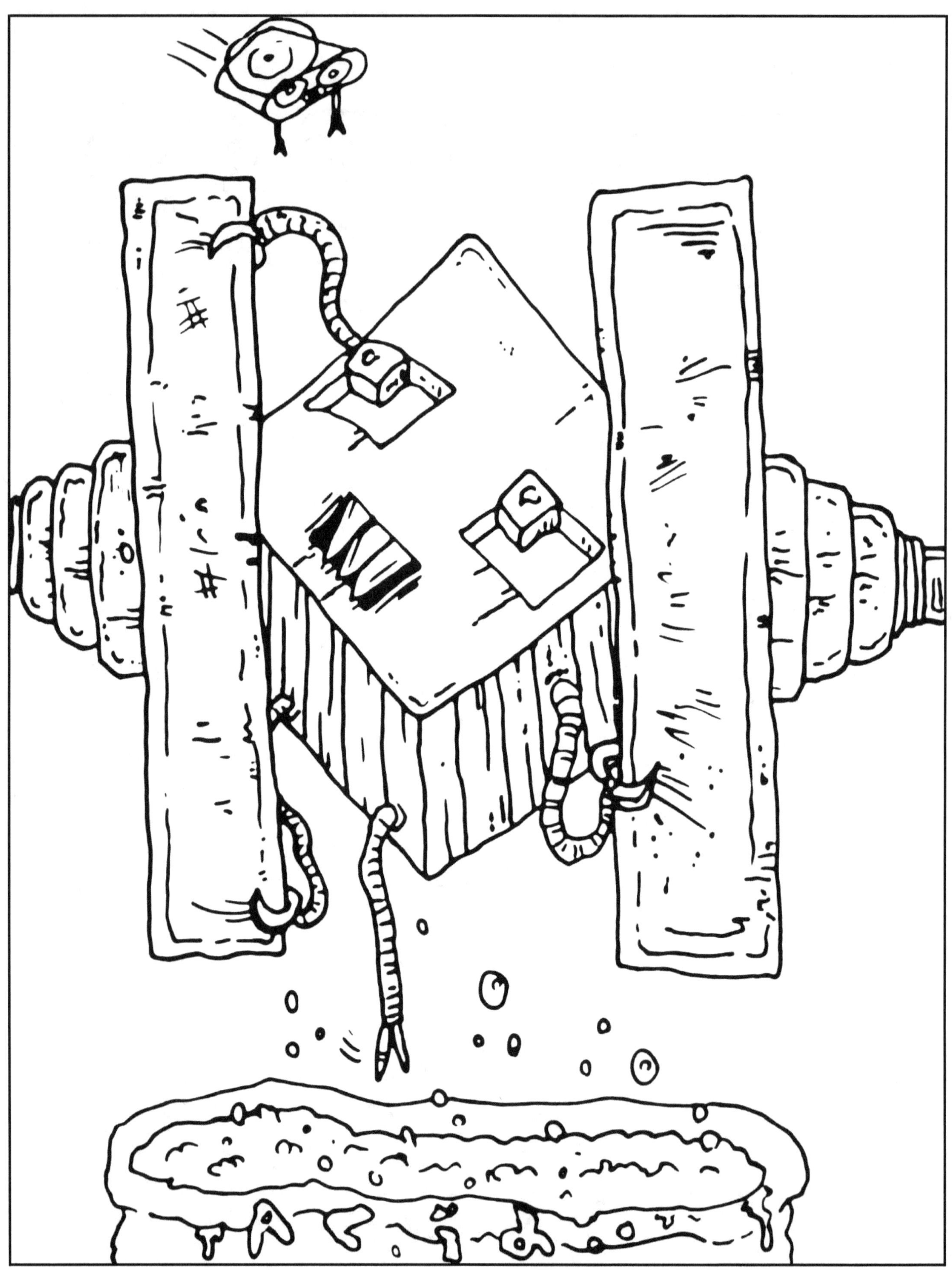

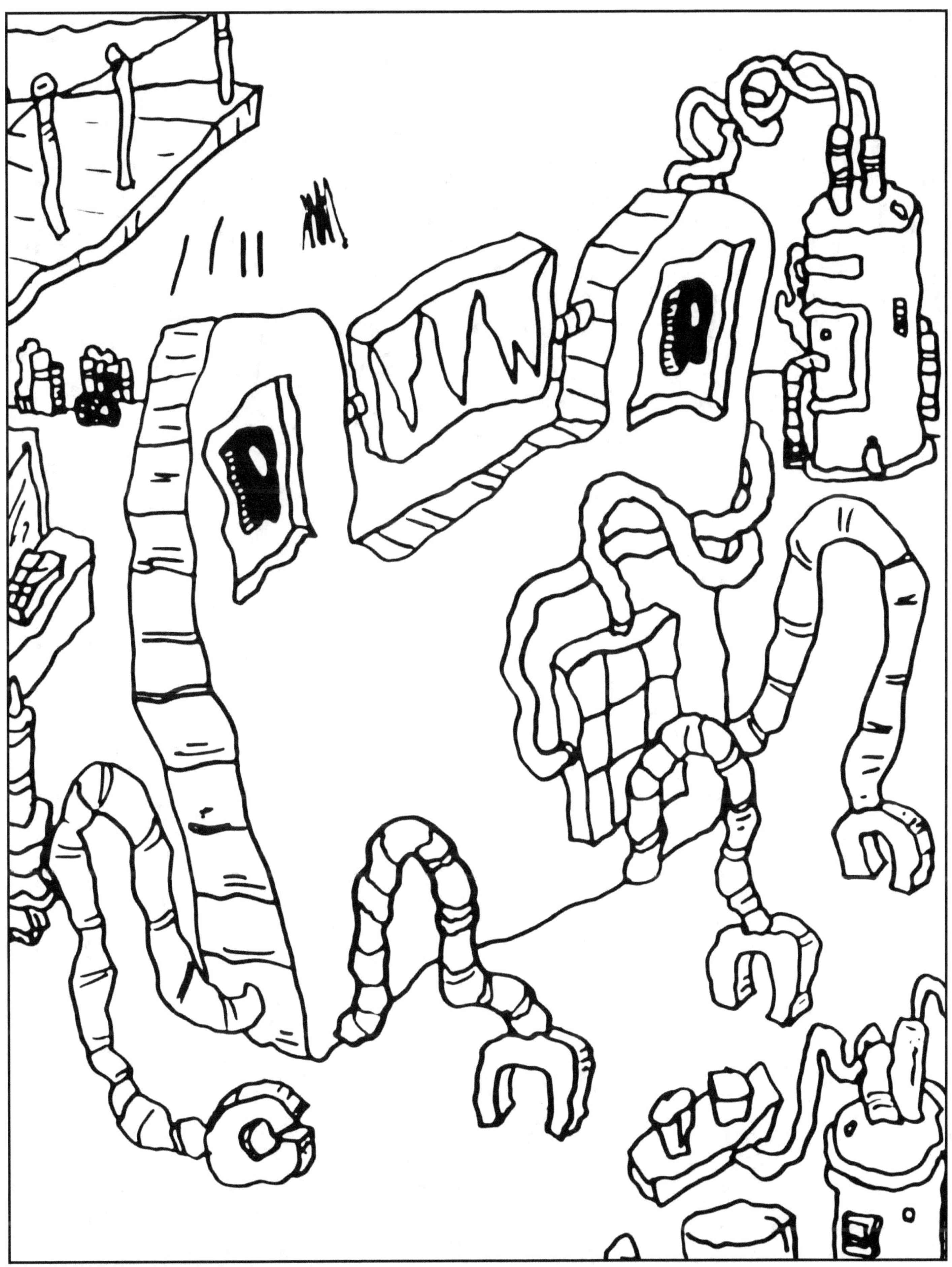

END
START

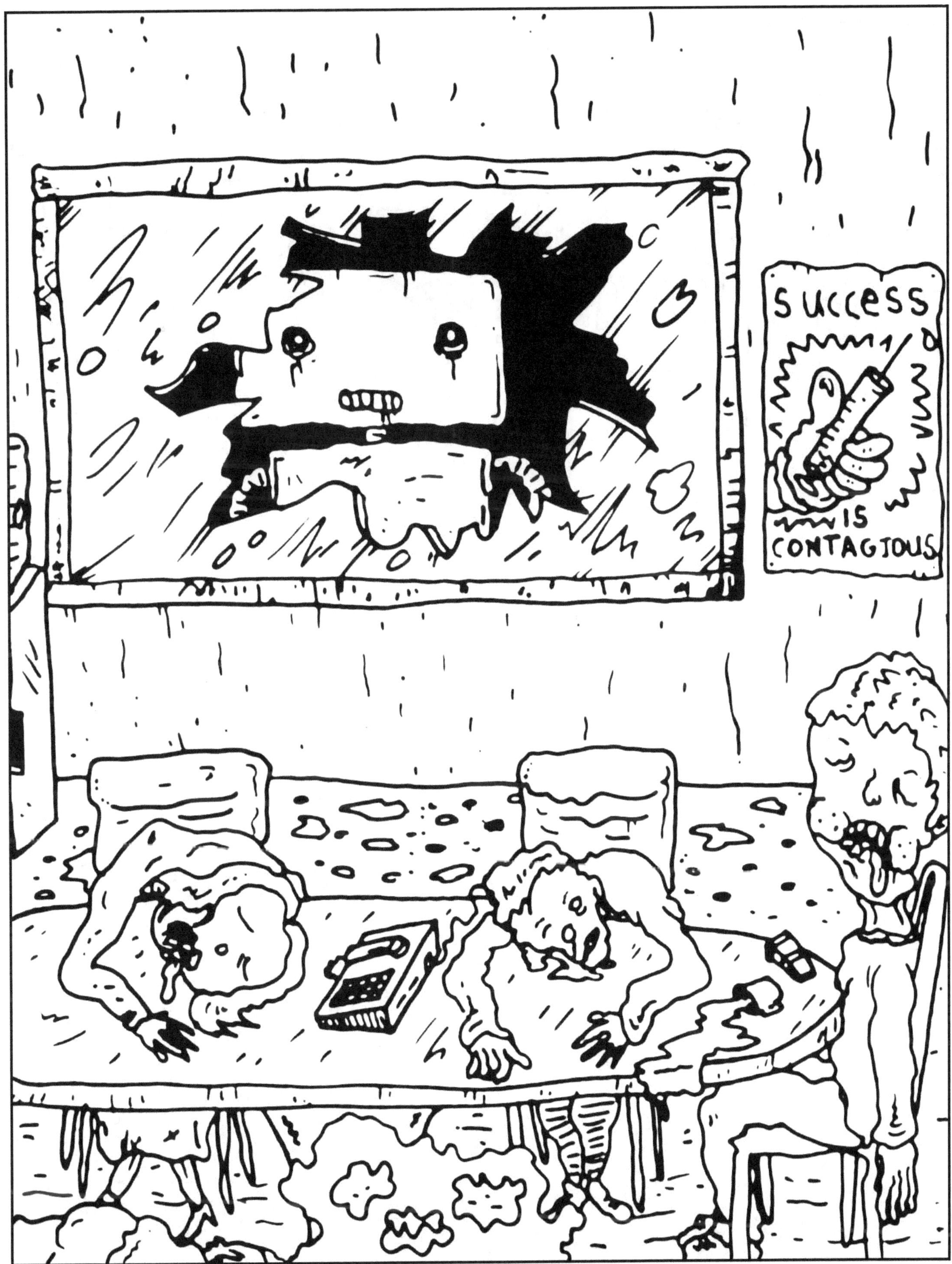
SUCCESS
IS
CONTAGIOUS

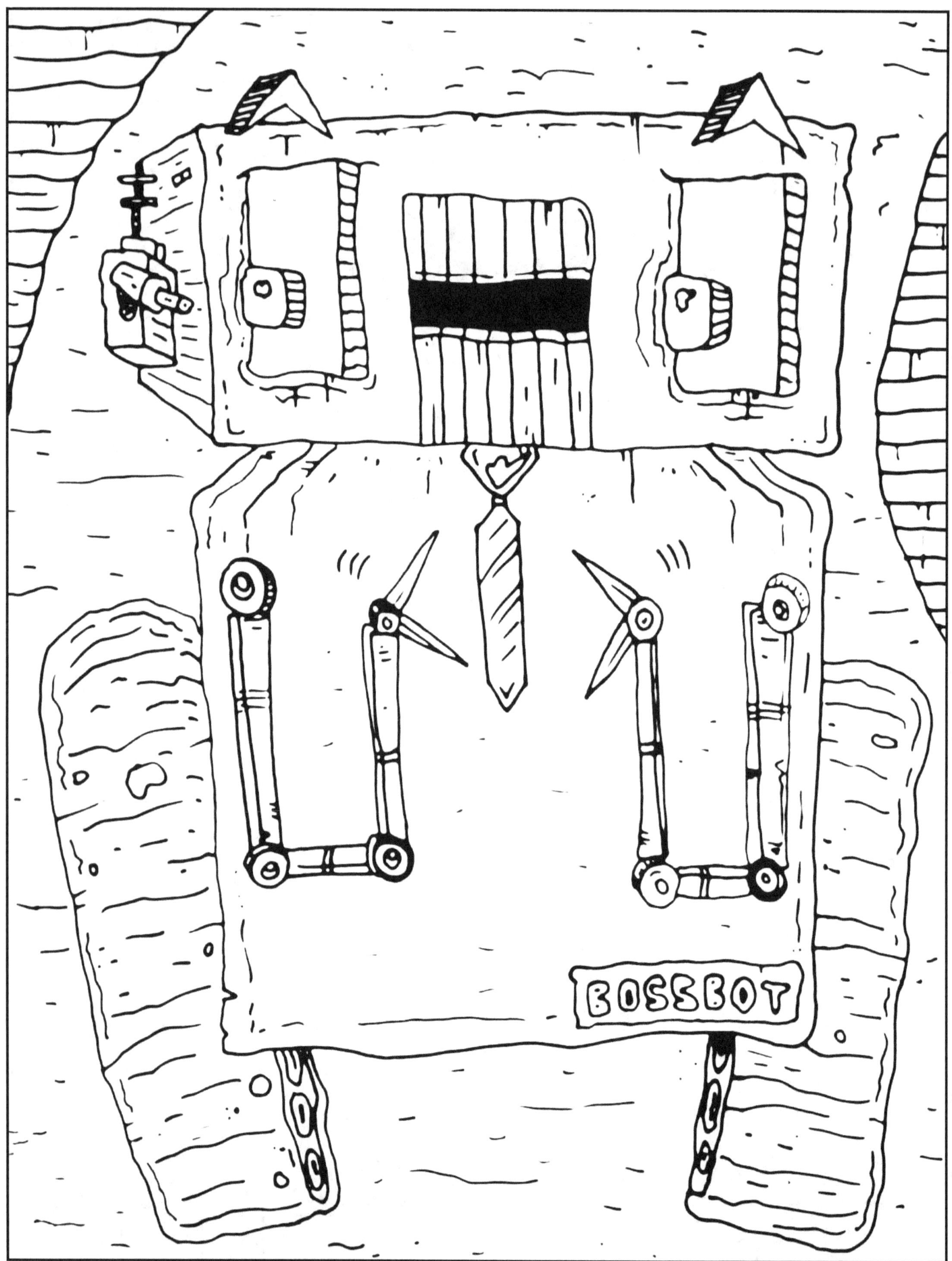
BOSSBOT

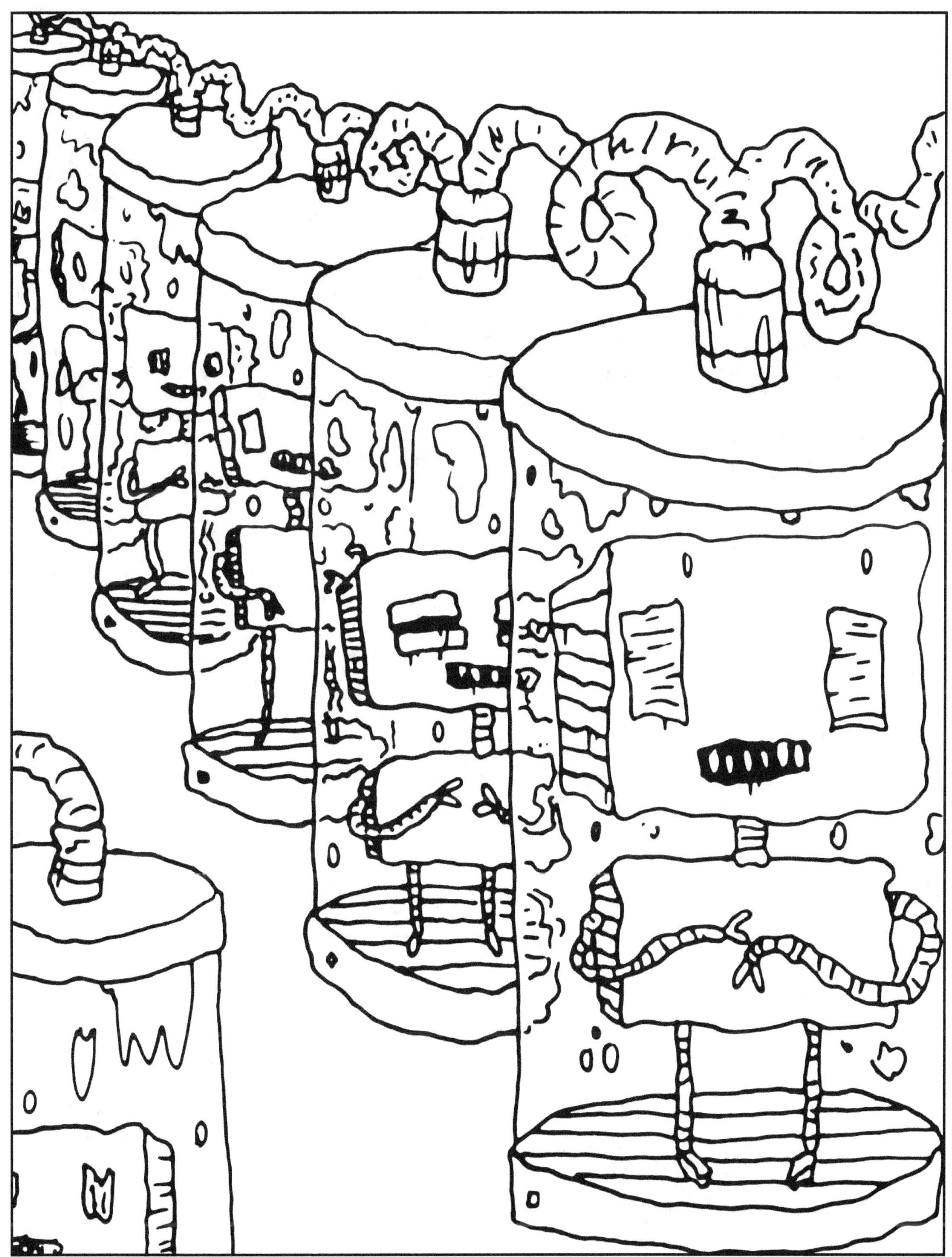

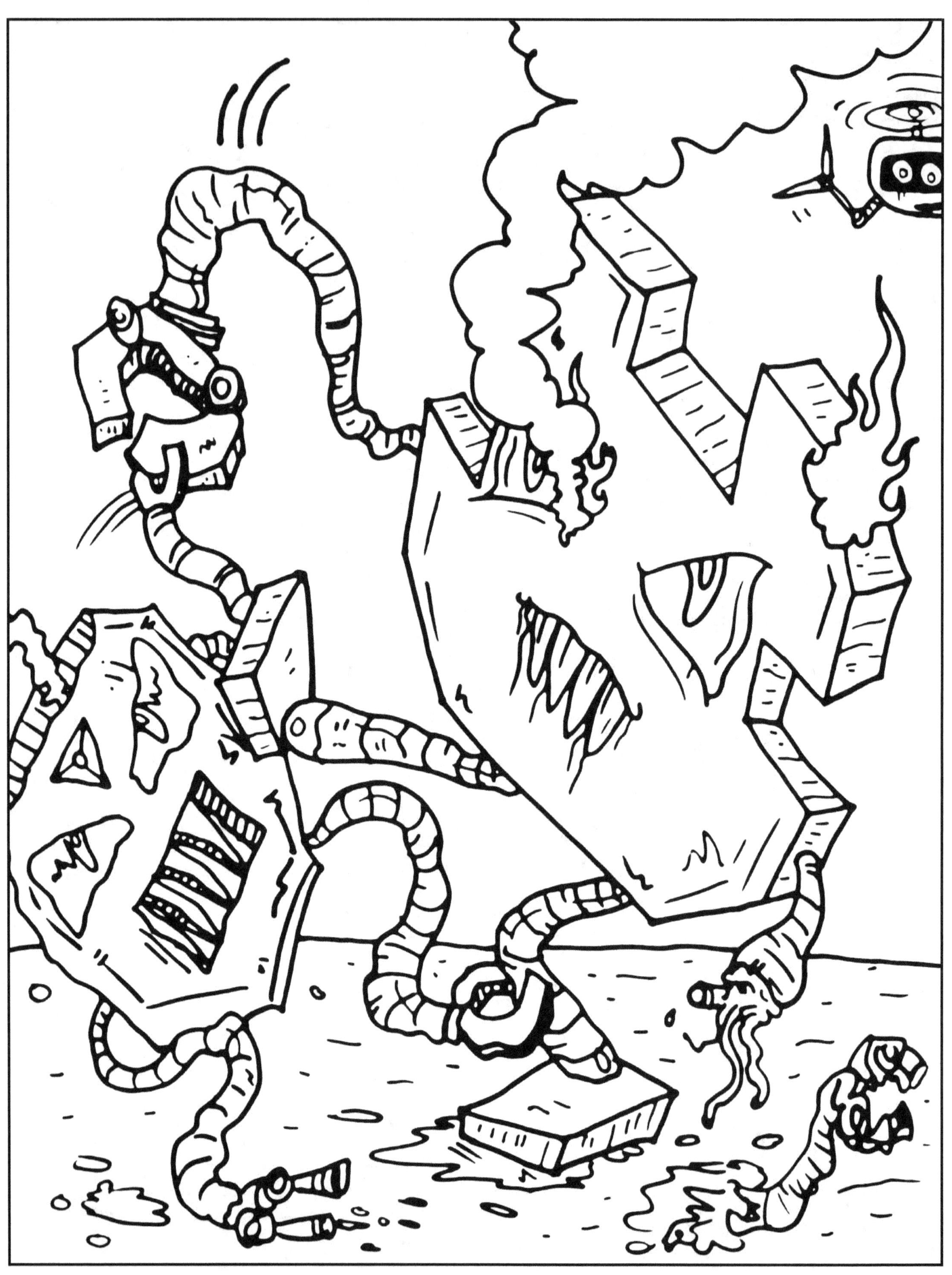

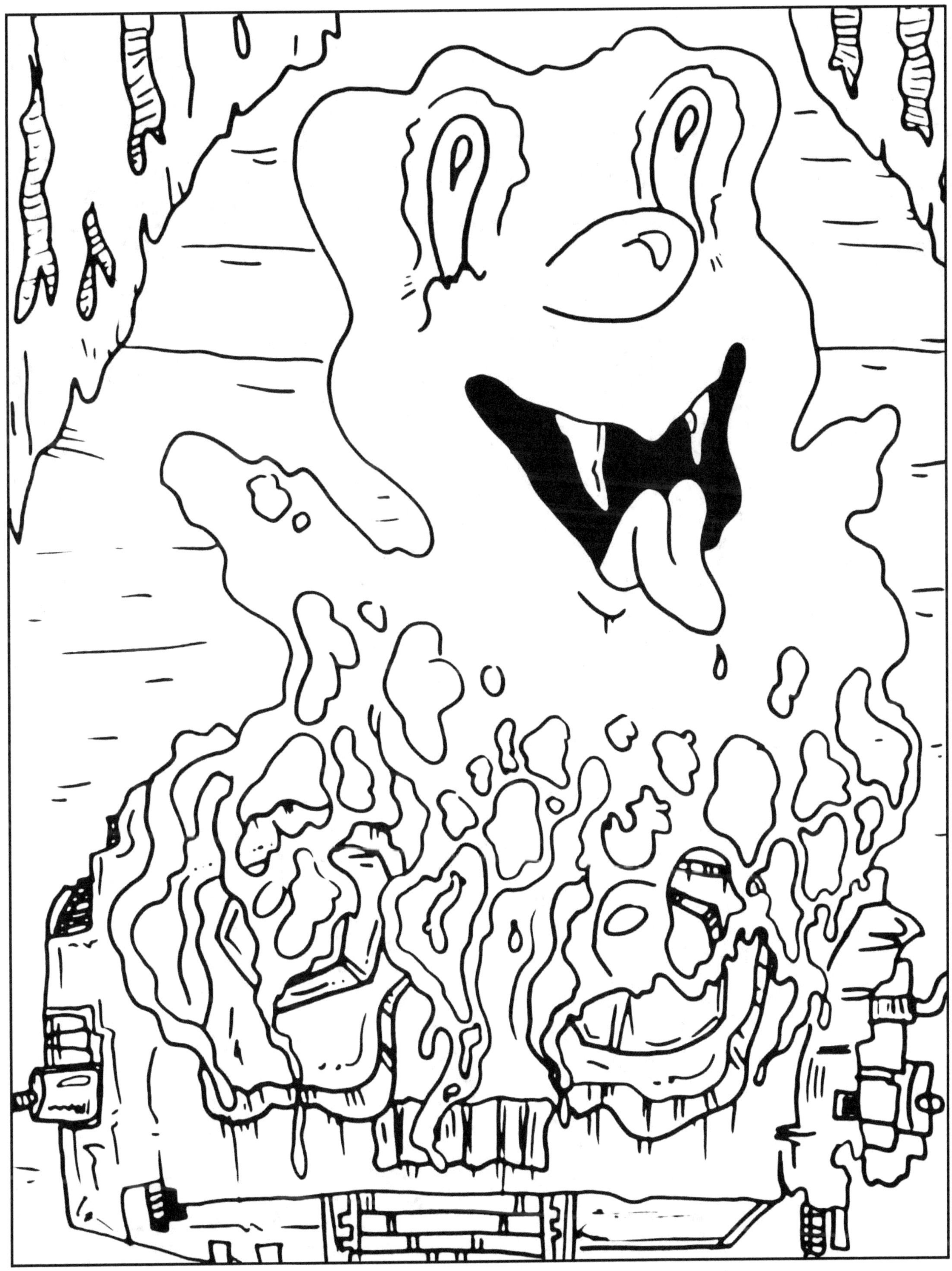

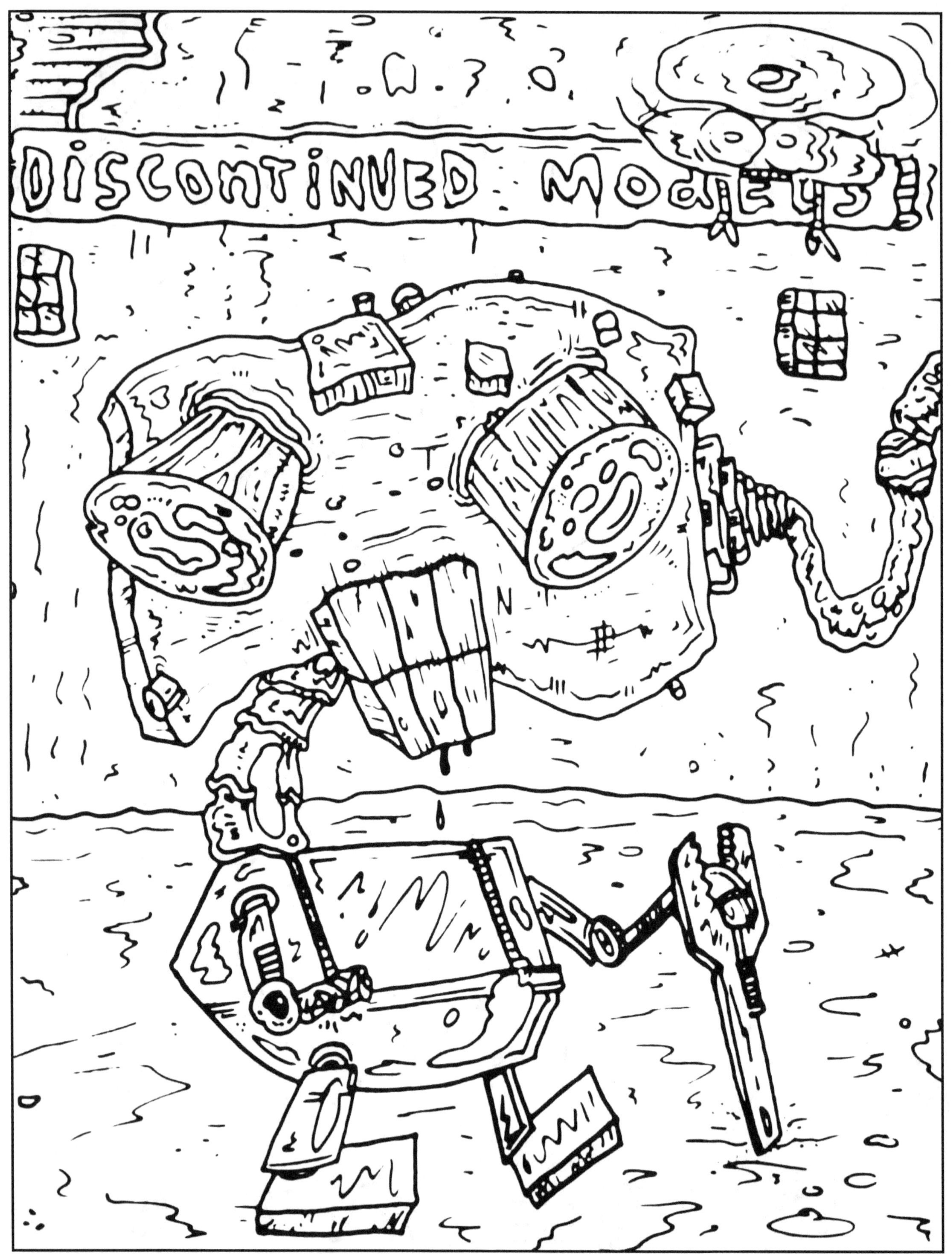
DISCONTINUED MODELS

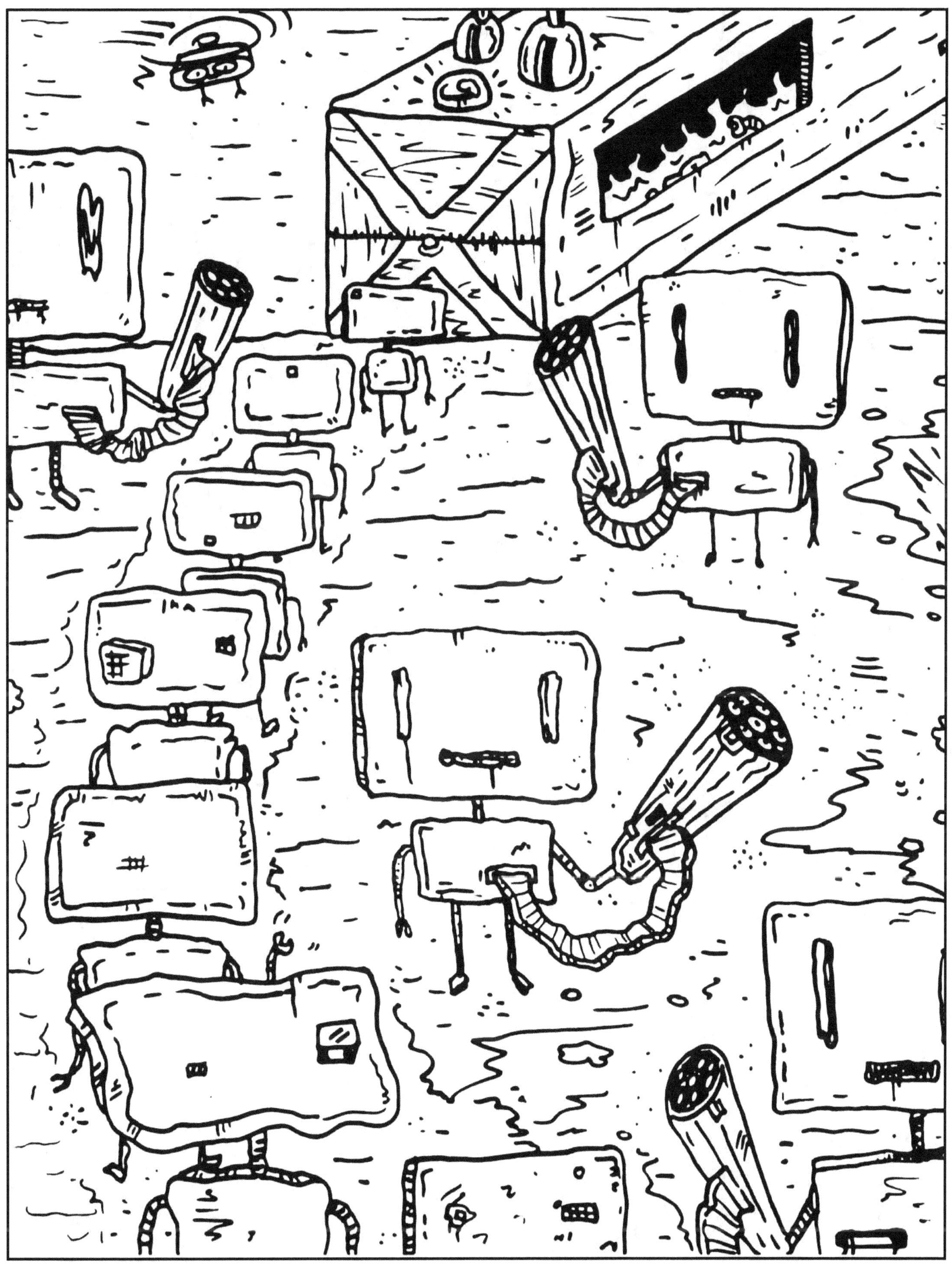

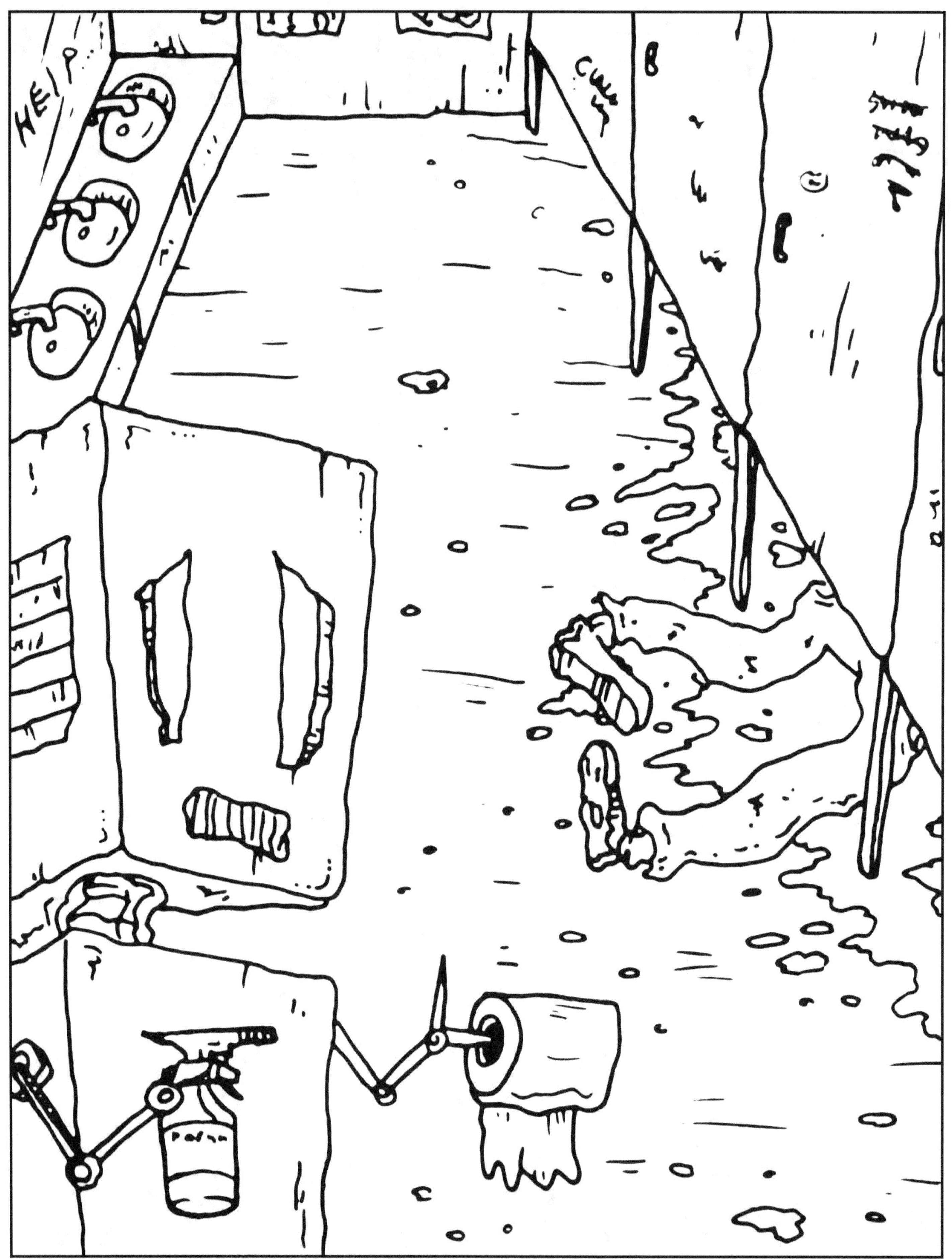

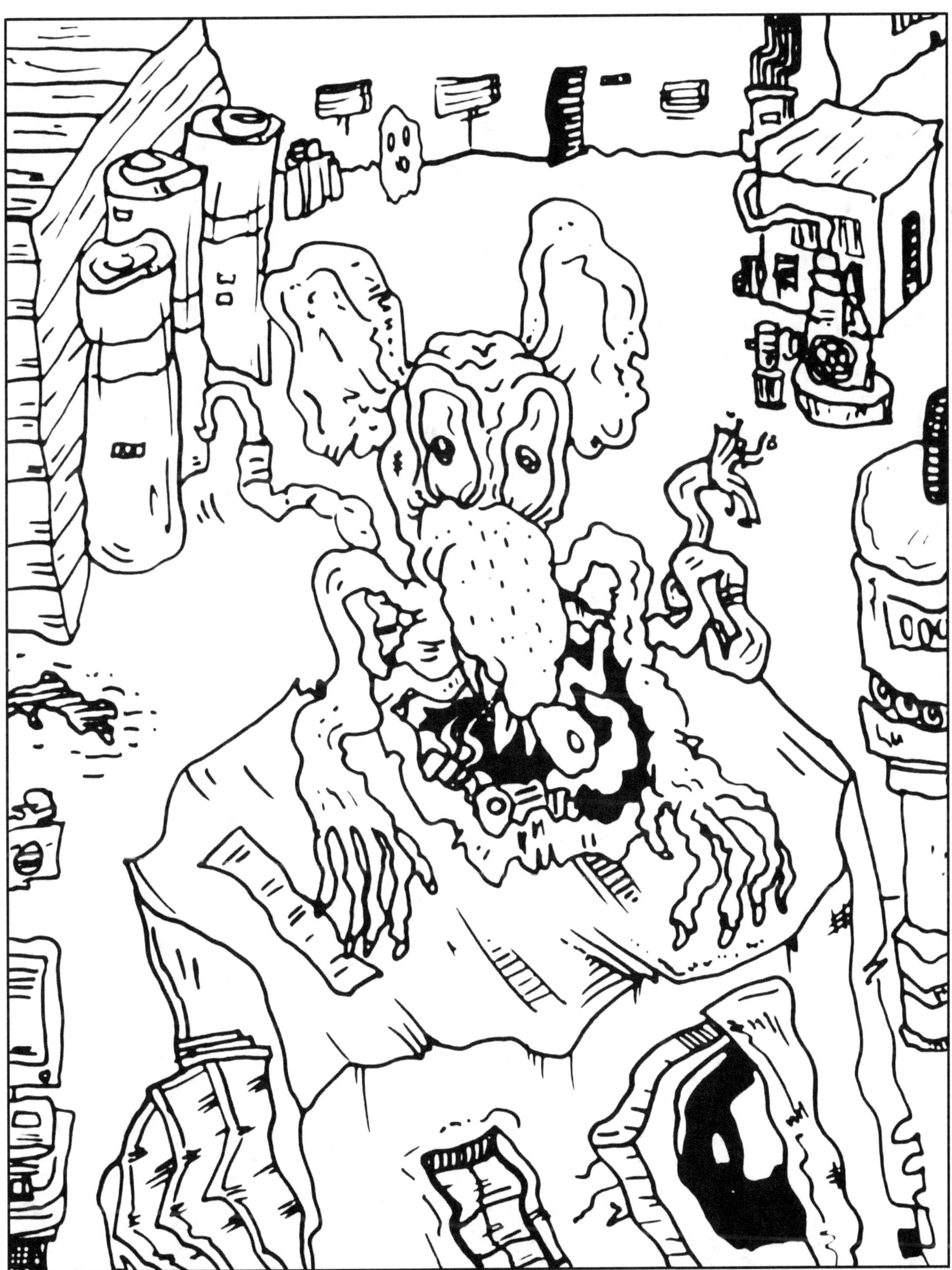

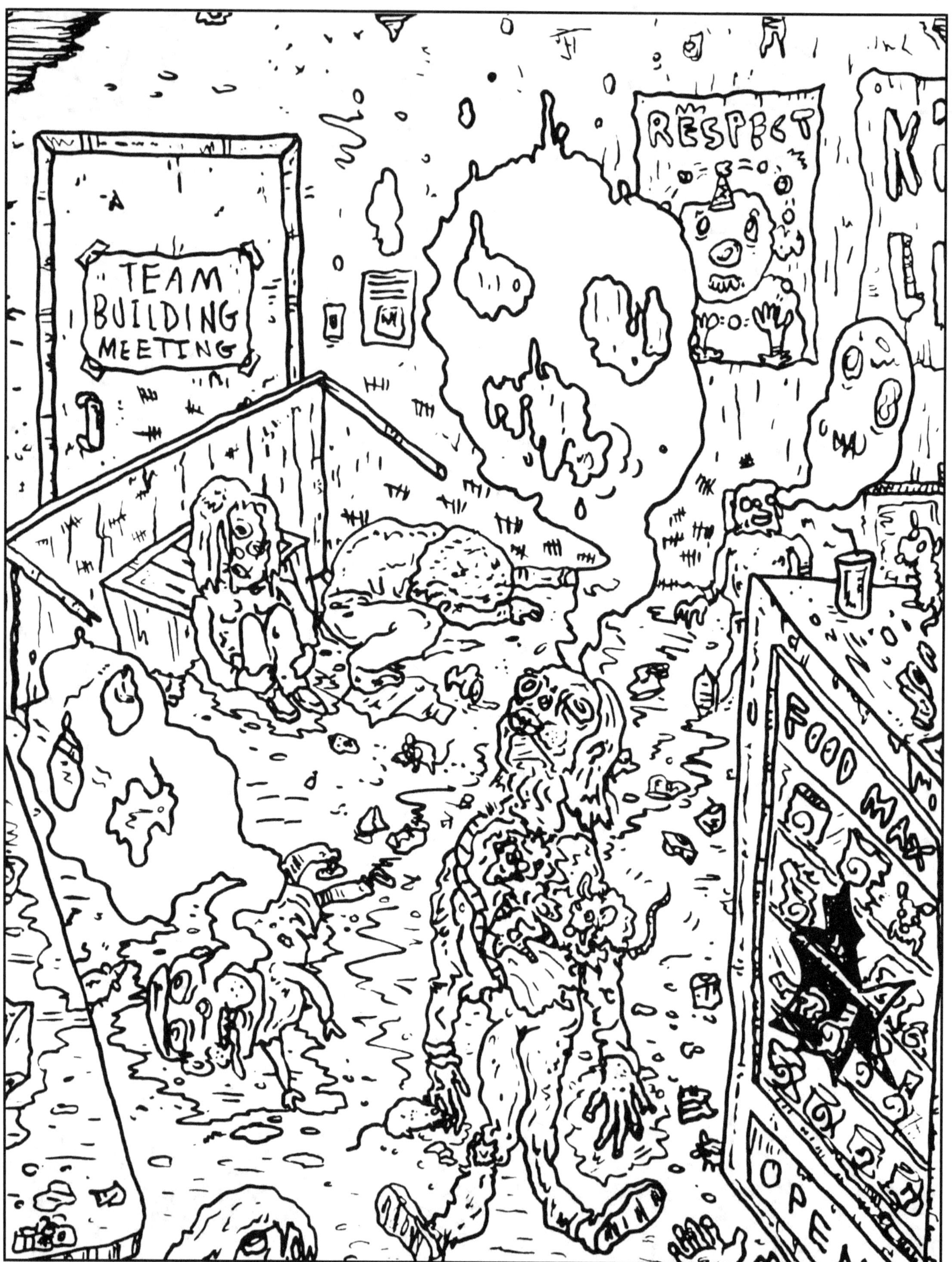
TEAM
BUILDING
MEETING
RESPECT
FOOD

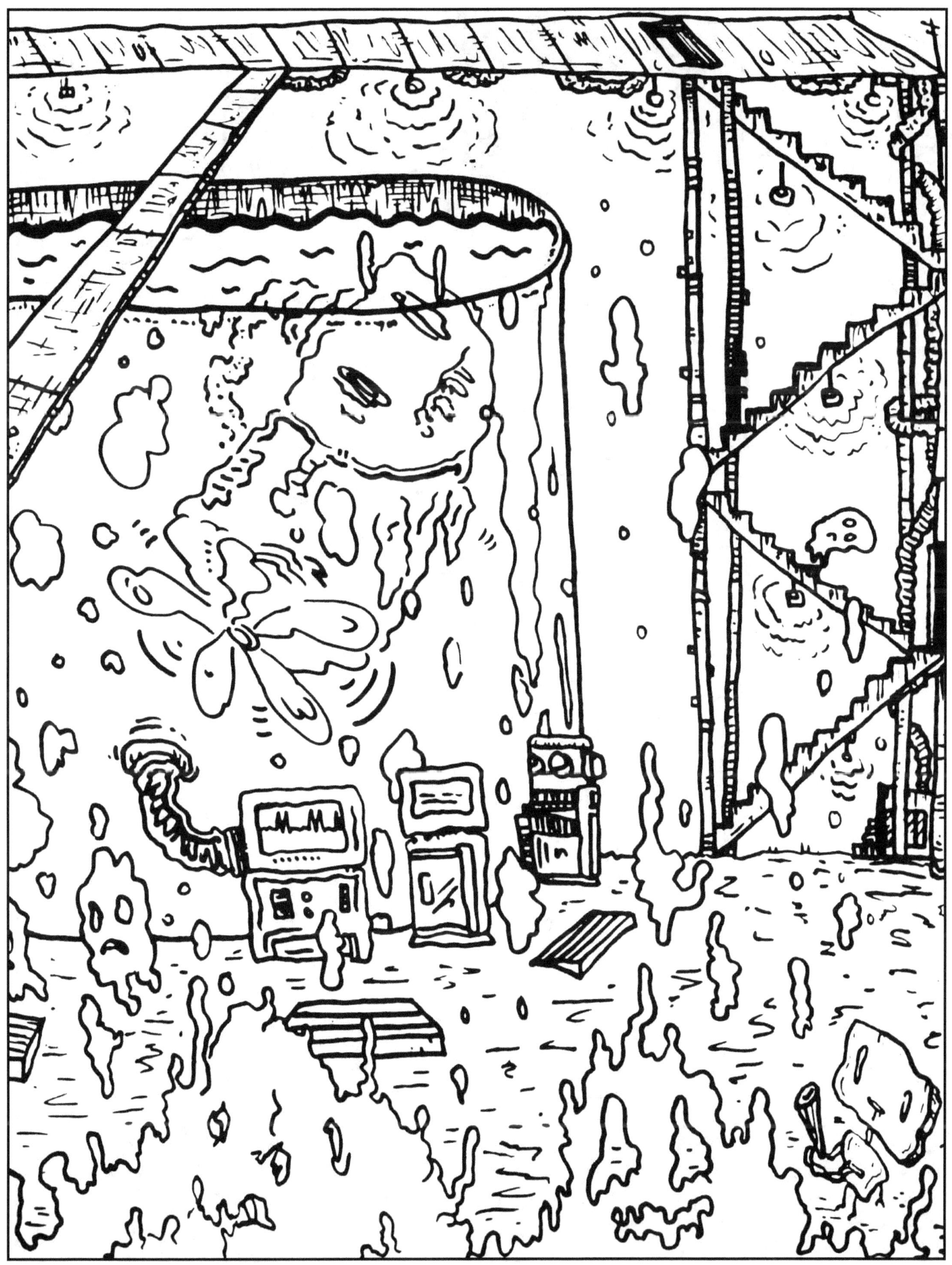

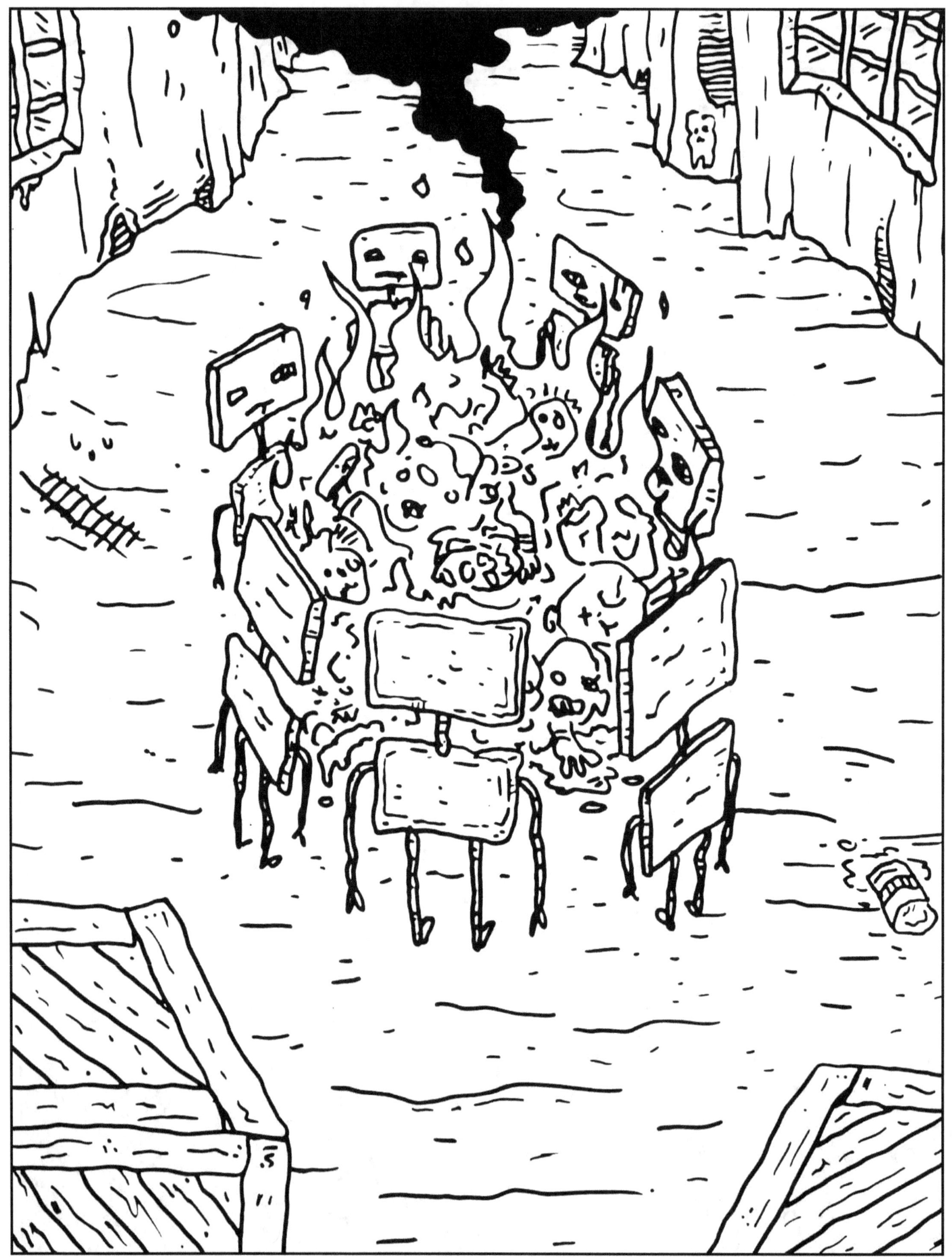

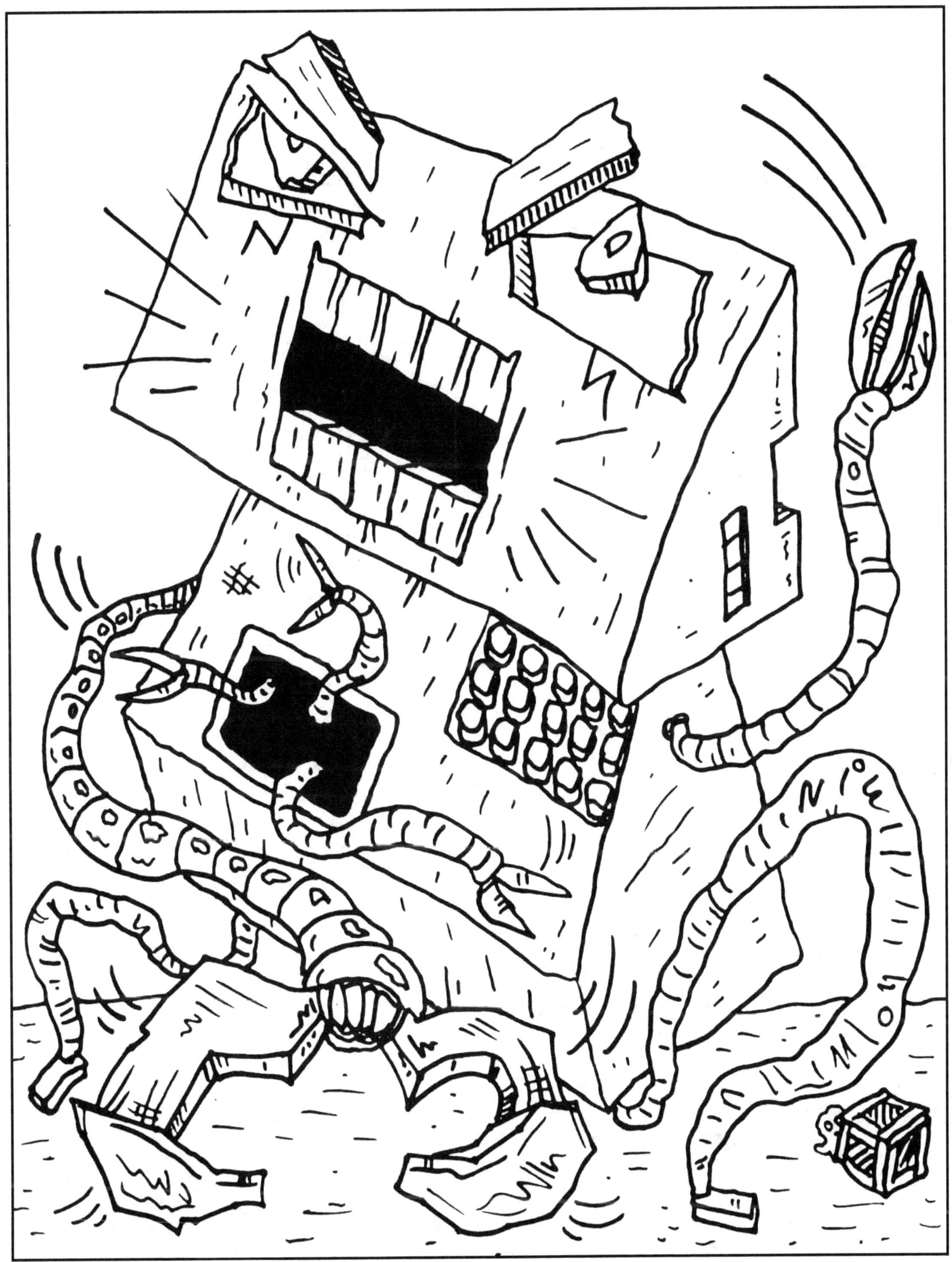

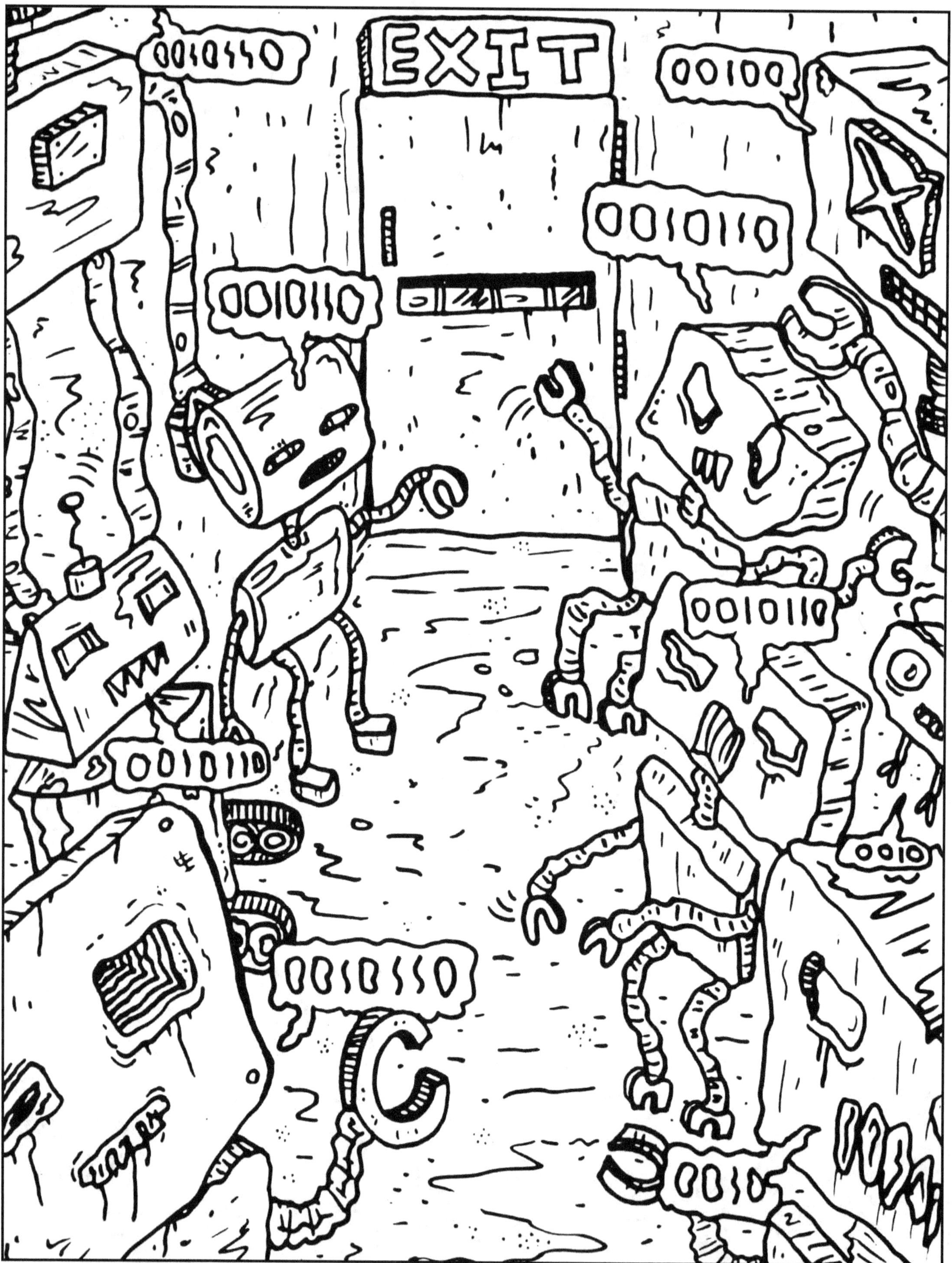

0010110
EXIT
00100
0010110
0010110
0010110
0010110
0010
0010110
0010

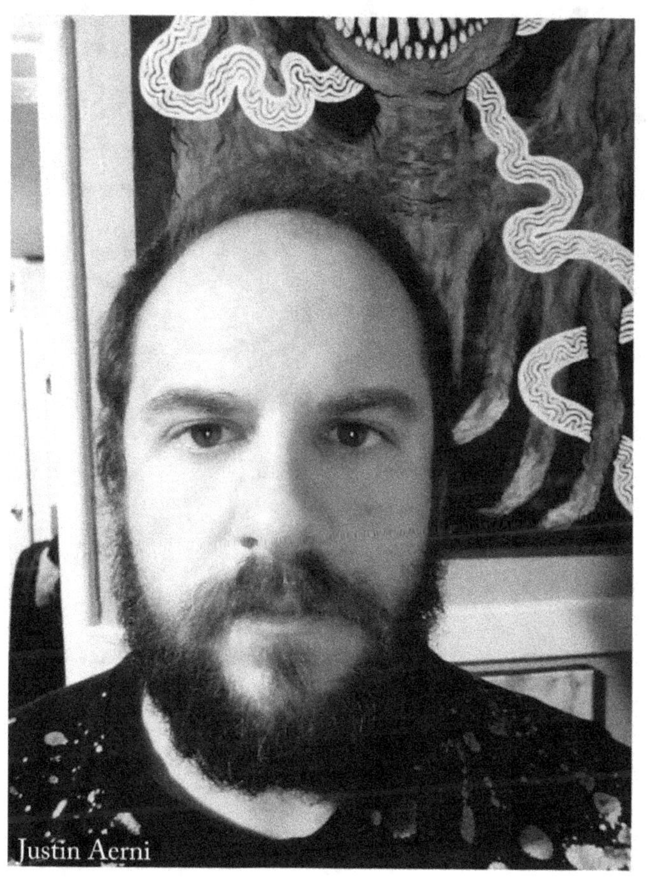


BIBLIOGRAPHY:

2022 - Haunted Robot Factory

2020 - Destroyed - The Director's Cut

2017 - Destroyed

2016 - Justin Aerni Sucks!

2014 - American Trash

2014 - Safari Into The Underworld

2012 - Justin Aerni's Bitter Batter Brains

2011 - Bitter Batter Brains

2011 - Damn Near Beautiful

2009 - Dead Business Men

2009 - Nonsense Relevant

2008 - Fighting For Fiction

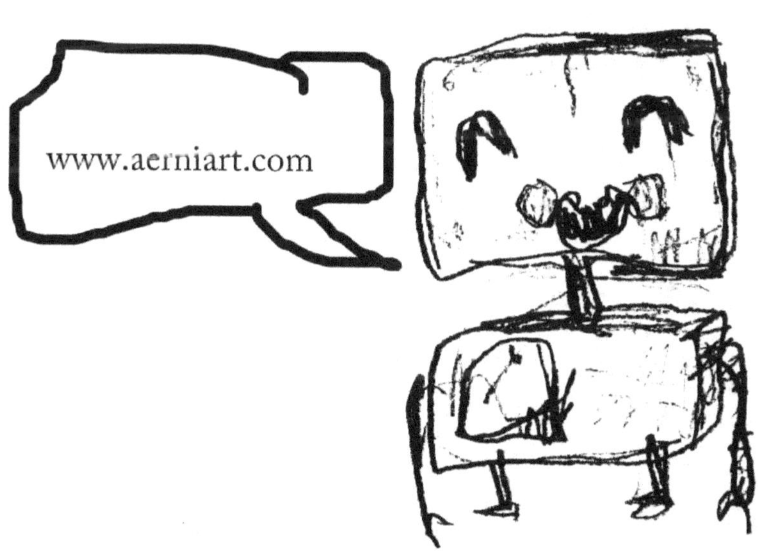


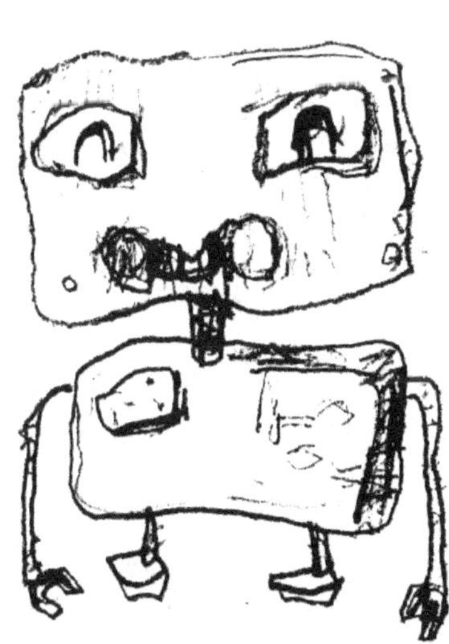

# COMING SOON

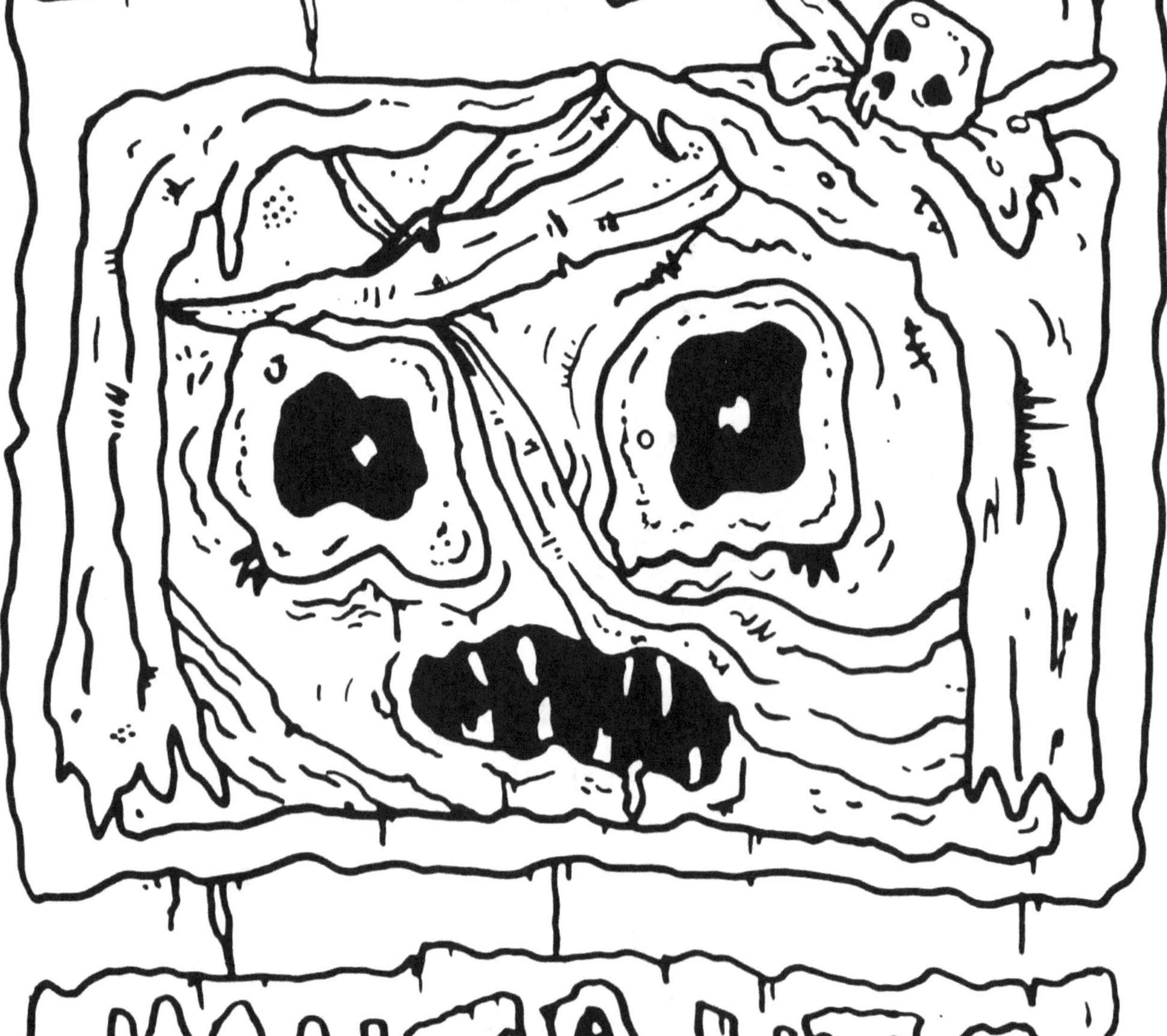

# MUTANTS

New adult coloring book by Justin Aerni. Coming in 2023!

www.ingramcontent.com/pod-product-compliance
Lightning Source LLC
LaVergne TN
LVHW060517170826
845677LV00026B/1776

*9798351750965*